UNSTOPPABLE WILLPOWER

HOW TO BE MOTIVATED AND CHANGE YOUR LIFE

BY SMART READS

Free Audiobook

ABOUT SMARTREADS

Choose Smart Reads and get smart every time. Smart Reads sorts through all the best content and condenses the most helpful information into easily digestible chunks.

We design our books to be short, easy to read and highly informative. Leaving you with maximum understanding in the least amount of time.

Smart Reads aims to accelerate the spread of quality information so we've taken the copyright off everything we publish and donate our material directly to the public domain. You can read our uncopyright below.

We believe in paying it forward and donate 5% of our net sales to Pencils of Promise to build schools, train teachers and support child education.

To limit our footprint and restore forests around the globe we are planting a tree for every 10 hardcover books we sell.

Thanks for choosing Smart Reads and helping us help the planet.

Sincerely,

Travis & the Smart Reads Team

TABLE OF CONTENTS

INTRODUCTION

Ever find yourself promising that you'll go to the gym at the start of the New Year? That this year will the one where you'll lose all your excess weight for sure and get in shape? How many times have you followed through on it?

Or did you end up stopping after a few weeks saying, "Oh, my body just isn't built for this. I'll have to figure some other way to get in shape." But then of course, never do. Then your goals become buried in your list of to do's and you feel even more miserable about not following through.

Rest assured, you're not the only one who goes through this. In fact, almost every person feels that at some point they lacked the motivation and willpower to follow through on a goal.

Willpower is crucial if you want to make good on an objective you've set - an objective that at first seems hard and which may cause you a degree of pain, such as giving up on your favorite food so that you can lose weight.

Willpower can change your life around. It can be the difference between failure, mediocrity and ultimate success.

Every single person, including you, all carries some willpower. It's just that each individual has different amounts. If you feel you don't have enough power, then here's your chance to learn how to make it stronger.

To achieve your dreams and live the life you want, you need unrelenting willower. In this book, you'll explore the mysteries of willpower, and how you can build your reserves so they become unstoppable.

CHAPTER 1: WHAT MOTIVATES YOU

Until you identify what motivates you, you'll struggle to build up your willpower.
As mentioned, each person is motivated by different things. And there are different situations that call for variations of motivation.

What motivates you to achieve a goal will not be the same thing that motivates your partner, friend or coworker in achieving theirs. In this chapter, you'll learn several motivations that could improve your willpower.

The most popular motivations will be addressed separately, but you might find that some of your preferred motivations are a mixed bag. For example, you might claim you want to write a self-help guide to help people, when the reality is that you want to make money from your writing.

Two different motivations, but until you identify which one is yours, you'll struggle to make a start.

Approval
Approval is a big deal. Approval can change the way you act, the way you dress, the things you say, and the goals you set. As kids, approval matters. And even now as adults, it continues to inform people's behavior and actions. People seek approval from others - they want others to like them, and to see them in a positive light.

For example, let's say you want to gain favor with your boss. If he asks you to work late tonight, you're going to say "yes" because you believe he'll have a more favorable feeling towards you. Or maybe because you want your colleagues to think you're doing well, and setting a good example at work.

The problem with motivations of this type is that it can cause you to behave in unhealthy ways if you're not careful. If you keep doing things to please other people, it's going to mean you're putting their needs before your own.

Money

Imagine doing a job you dislike? Imagine getting up each morning at 6 AM to go and work for a boss you hated? Imagine working 9 hours straight, even though you hated the work and your colleagues? Why would anyone do that? It sounds like madness.

Unfortunately, this is an everyday occurrence. Many people lead this kind of life. Why do they do it? Because they're motivated by money. Put simply, the only reason they do jobs they don't like is for money. There is no other reason, right?

Sometimes, money isn't even enough to keep people in jobs they dislike. The fast-food industry has a high turnover because the hours are lousy, the pay is rubbish, and the customers are often insensitive.

If you listen to what the cognitive dissonance theory says, if the reward doesn't seem proportionate to the amount of effort you're putting in, you'll either quit or somehow convince yourself the pay is justified and that it's good enough.

A desire for money and to survive is what keeps millions of people in jobs around the world.

Love
Meat Loaf once sang he would do anything for love. And it's true that most people would do many things for love. Love can even drive some people to murder! Love makes people do crazy things. It takes them out of their comfort zone. It emboldens and gives people courage to stand up for something they never imagined themselves standing up for when they were younger.

Hate
Hate can drive people to do things, too. Individuals who hate the current state of their life would be motivated to go out and do something to change it. Often, it's only once they've associated enough pain with something that they're finally compelled to take action.

Take smoking as an example. People who smoke know it's bad for them. They want to quit smoking to save their health, but they don't have the willpower. "I'll quit when I'm 30," they might say.

But when something bad happens to them, such as a nasty health scare, it can be enough to shake them that they're finally compelled to act and quit smoking. All of a sudden, they hate smoking and what it's doing to them. They want to make a change. As you can see, hate can be used as a force for good.

Revenge

Are you sometimes driven to take action by thoughts of revenge? It's odd to admit this but it's a common motivation for most people.

Spite and revenge is obviously bad. But revenge can be a great motivator, especially when it comes to restoring justice. However, it's important to figure out whether your thirst for vengeance is just and proportionate to the harm already dished out, or whether you're acting out of callous spite and should instead let bygones be bygones.

Fear

Fear is a great motivator. Fear of being homeless drives many people to find work. Fear of being lonely drives others to find romantic partners. Fear of being overweight and chronically sick when older drives people to eat healthy today.

When you fear getting fat and unattractive, you exercise. When you fear on missing out on the good life, you take calculated risks. When you fear missing out on you one chance with that girl at the bar, you go over and talk to her.

Fear of Missing Out (FOMO) is a huge motivator. Marketers know this all too well, which is why they'll often remind you in advertising campaigns that other people are enjoying their product while you're still missing out!

CHAPTER 2: UNDERSTANDING WHY YOU HAVE NO WILLPOWER

Willpower Depletion Explained

When you pound your muscles until they're worn down, exhausted and can't function as well as you'd like them to, they have reached their point of depletion.

Forcing them to go beyond this point without letting them recover isn't going to "build their character" and make them tougher. It's only going to break them and drain them of all their energy and resources.

Willpower works in much the same way. Just like your muscles, you can only flex a set amount of your willpower in a single day. And once you've used your quota, you've reached what is called willpower depletion. If you attempt to go beyond this point, you'll fail.

What Depletes Willpower?

There are a few things that can deplete your willpower. They vary from person to person, but they might include:

- Impressing your date
- Sitting through an awfully dull meeting
- Giving up specific food items
- Getting up early in the morning
- Exercising even though you absolutely hate it

Essentially, you can name any new thing that you don't want to do. It's going to take up a LOT of your willpower reserves. As such, what's important here is not how much total willpower you get through in a single day. What's important is you choose your fights carefully. In other words, you choose where to expend your willpower with great care.

A colossal expectation is assuming you can do so much straight away. Not even so much, but everything.

A great example of this includes people who decide they want to go into business to get rich. They don't want to have to wait 3-5 years before the money starts to roll in. They want it right now. And when they realize they can't have it right away, they lose a lot of heart. They are sapped of energy.

People like this are always in the state of willpower depletion. And the more they remain in this perpetual state of willpower depletion, the weaker their willpower becomes.

Cutting out specific food items cold turkey is drastic and extreme. But as long as you've got a realistic plan, it could work out. However, if you don't have a realistic plan, it's only going to weaken your willpower until it eventually snaps altogether.

Adversaries of Willpower
Whenever an army goes to war, they must know their enemy. And as you fight for what unstoppable

willpower, you too must know where your adversaries are because they will surely be there.

The problem is that even if your motivators are strong, they can be set up against a much stronger enemy of willpower. As such, no matter how great you think the motivator is, it still can't compel you to take action because the adversaries of willpower are too strong.

Let's take a look at what shape these adversaries might take:

Hunger
How many irrational decisions does hunger cause you to make? There's a story about the new vegetarian who was invited to a friend's party. She was quite hungry but found out the party didn't serve any vegetarian meals at all.

Even though she wanted to quit eating animal products, her hunger won out and she ended up eating a steak, which was served for the guests. In the end, her hunger was her enemy and it eventually won over her willpower.

Fatigue
Another common adversary of willpower is fatigue. It can hit you at the most unexpected and unwanted moments. Maybe you literally can't wake up at all day, despite having so much work to do. Sometimes fatigue creeps up on you mid-afternoon after you've had your lunch.

There are a few things that can cause fatigue, such as stress, lack of sleep and poor diet. And when fatigue hits; it can prevent you from working on your goals. You're just too tired to even try. When dieting and fatigue hits, it can make you veer off course. Instead of rustling up another healthy meal tonight, you order a takeaway because it's easier.

When you're working on a new business idea and fatigue hits, you decide to skip a day and watch cat videos instead. Fatigue causes people to lose time and sight of their goals. Fatigue can be fixed, though. All you need to do is root out the cause of it, and work on it.

Stress
Everyone gets stressed. However, stress is not good if you need more willpower. Instead, it can be destructive.

One of the reasons for this is that when you are stressed, you adopt a fight or flight mentality. Willpower, on the other hand, requires you to take a step back for a moment and make a plan.

When stressed, you will find it hard to sit down and calmly map a plan for how you can resolve the current situation you're in. Most people enter panic mode and can't think straight. Some may reach for a bottle of wine. Others might quit their job. Others go to the doctor and start taking medication.

During stressful situations, people don't think in normal terms. They don't act rationally, and they don't always do the things that are in their best interests.

Seeing the bigger picture becomes difficult and people feel suffocated. Stress is a big enemy to willpower and can take you off course.

Self-Criticism
Studies have highlighted that being overly critical of yourself can dramatically weaken your willpower.

Often, people prefer to criticize themselves with scathing words instead of actively preventing themselves from self-indulging. And the more heavily they criticize, the worse they feel.

It's similar to "comfort eating." People will comfort eat after a bad day when they feel they've been treated badly. How can you remedy self-criticism? You could try giving self-compassion a go.

Self-compassion is the opposite of self-criticism. Instead of being unnecessarily harsh on yourself, you go easy on yourself. You admit your weaknesses but you give yourself the encouragement needed to get over them.

Take a piece of paper and write down words of encouragement to yourself. The more you do this, the more you'll be able to approach things with a positive, can-do attitude.

Blind, Unwavering Optimism

Nearly everyone is told to be more optimistic. But what if you're too optimistic? Or what if your optimism is misguided?

Blind, unwavering optimism does not fortify your willpower. Everyone needs a bit of a reality check to keep himself or herself grounded. Any goals you choose to focus on must be dreams that are achievable.

Moreover, blind faith alone cannot get you to where you want to be. You can't say "I'm never going to snack after 10PM!" and expect that to be that.

You may have said this mantra with lots of enthusiasm, and maybe you believe in your resolve. But unless you put things in place that will help you to achieve this goal (such as throwing all your snacks into the garbage), your leap of faith won't be enough to get you over the finish line.

CHAPTER 3: BREAKING BAD HABITS AND FORMING GOOD ONES

Habits can define your reality. Why do you do the things you do? Why does your wife eat cake after almost every meal? Why do you watch the NBA every Friday night? You might say, "because these things are awesome." They possibly are. But usually the reason you keep doing the same thing over and over again is because they've become a habit.

Cognitive unconsciousness controls people's breathing, balancing, walking and so on. Breathing isn't something you think about most of the time. In fact, the mention of it just now has probably brought it to your attention for the first time in a long time. And what about the other, less obvious things that cognitive unconscious controls, such as the way you switch between pedals when driving? Or how about when you brush your teeth each morning and night without fail?

These are things you don't even think about. You just do them. You don't need to be reminded that if you didn't brush your teeth twice a day you'd end up with rotting teeth. You're conditioned to brush.

Habits make your days more efficient. You don't have to stop and think about something. You just do it. Many of your habits are formed during childhood and formative years. You've likely kept the useful ones including bad ones.

Habits are formed like this: each time you do something new; your brain neurons form synapses. Every time you repeat an action, these synapses grow in strength.

It was Aristotle who said that, "We are what we do repeatedly."

Bad habits are developed the same way. You've been doing them for years; they've become part of your nature and who you are. Often, you don't even notice you're doing them.

If someone says to you, "Why do you always do that?" you might even ask, "Do what?"

Habits are hard to break. And when you are trying to break a habit, stress becomes your enemy. Imagine if you're trying to give up smoking but then you have a bad day. You feel stressed and you do the only thing you know will make you feel better right now - you pull out a cigarette.

Just like the habits you've picked up over your lifetime, they become part of who you are including any new habits you want to pick up. If you want to lose weight, write a novel, become a long distance runner or become a vegetarian, you can do all of these things through the power of habit. It's totally possible.

Why Habits > Willpower

As Aristotle pointed out over 2,000 years ago, **excellence is a habit - as opposed to an act.** Excellence is achieved when you have mastered something.

How do you master something? By doing it repeatedly.

Habits can be your best weapon, or they can be your worse liability. They can create your dream life, or your worst nightmare. It's entirely up to you. But know this - the power is within your hands to decide if habits are going to improve your life or worsen it.

The choice is yours. You have to realize and internalize this fact:

Willpower will not defeat a deeply embedded habit.

Willpower is unstoppable when it grows in power. It can be a colossal force for change. But willpower cannot help you achieve all your goals by itself. It needs help. Simply saying, "I can do this!" is not enough, despite what great motivators on social media tell you.

You've seen them. The guys who say you've got to "take action!" The guys who say if you're only going to do one thing today it's to get out of bed and tackle that one task you've been putting off for ages. All this sounds great, but by itself it's just not enough to get you the results you want.

Bad Habits > Willpower

Bad habits are yet another enemy of willpower. They're what people fall back into after they get distracted. You could be making great progress with something, but as soon as something knocks you out of your stride and causes you to waver, you fall back into those comforting bad habits once again. Maybe you'll pick up a cigarette, have a beer or order a greasy takeaway.

It all comes down to how you've trained your neural pathways down the years. Referring back to the story of the vegetarian earlier, she found it easy for the first few weeks. "I'm never going back to meat," she'd enthuse with pride. "I have no need." Why, then, did she return to meat every now and then? Why did she cave and ate meat? It's because she'd trained her neural pathways so intensely for so many years that it was impossible to just suddenly retrain them. She had a bad habit - eating meat, especially when she was stressed, didn't feel good, or she was lacking in choice.

On the other hand, there are people who manage to radically change their behavior and habits. If you go through Instagram, you've likely seen men and women showcasing their "before" and "after" pictures? Didn't they manage to kick their habit of overeating? Well, sure! But they didn't change their behaviors using just willpower alone. There were more ingredients. However, what's true is they all managed to kick their bad habits. And if they kicked theirs, you can kick yours - for good.

All you have to do is model yourself on someone else who has done what you're striving to do. The key thing all those individuals who kicked bad habits did is they found a new, healthy habit to replace the old bad one. The more your practice this replacement habit, the more it will become your brand new habit. It's all about getting your brain to learn a new neural pathway while phasing out the dated one you no longer want.

Think of it like letting go of an old friend in favor of a new life. You see the friend less and less as you begin to adapt to your new life. They're still getting drunk every Friday night while you're doing other things now. After a while, you might stop seeing them altogether and it no longer bothers you. You've got a new life with different interests. You've adapted.

To break a bad habit and replace it with a new one, you first have to figure out why you're susceptible to it, and when. When are you at your weakest? When does it come along and snare you? What are your triggers?

For many, their trigger is sheer boredom. They're bored, they need something to do, and the habit presents itself as an attractive option. It sits on their shoulder, smiles and says, "Pick me." The trick at this stage is to think of a healthier, better alternative.

Smokers might swap a cigarette with a hard boiled sweet. The smoking habit is still technically there, but it's been sublimated, so to speak. It looks slightly different, and is invariably healthier.

Good Habits

When you form a good habit instead of a bad one, it becomes the habit you fall back on when you're sick, stressed or otherwise not doing too great. It can automatically kick in especially when life throws you a sudden, unexpected curveball.

This book won't go into detail about why good habits are good for you. You already know why. Instead, it's important you gather some tips on how you can adopt these good habits for yourself.

Practice Makes Perfect

The phrase "practice makes perfect" is something most people have been told over and over again, and it's absolutely true. The more you practice something, the better you'll get at it.

The practicing doesn't just pertain to activities or skills you want to acquire. It's also true when trying to instill a new habit.

When you practice, you're creating new synapses so your brain becomes conditioned to your new behavior and the new habit becomes second nature. Eventually, your fingers will know exactly where to go on the guitar fret board as you play that Led Zeppelin solo. You no longer have to look!

Baby Steps

A lot of people make goals and expect to achieve them immediately. This is true for many aspiring entrepreneurs who are especially focused on all the money they could make instead of focusing on providing value and solving other people's problems. As such, they crave instant success and get massively disappointed when it isn't forthcoming.

Success at anything takes time, and you have to be focused on the incremental improvements. World-class sprinters work seriously hard all year-round just to shave $1/10^{th}$ of a second off their time. Imagine that, $1/10^{th}$ of a second! They know it's a small improvement, but they know how significant it is.

As you form new, better habits, you probably won't find them to stick straight away. Give them time. They will stick for you eventually.

Set Small Goals Each Day

To this end, it's a good idea to set small goals each day. Big goals look great at first. "I want to lose 30 pounds!" Sounds great!

At first, you're really pumped. You're on your way to a brand new life. But then you realize just how BIG this goal is. It's huge. It's unrealistic.

It's difficult to achieve massive goals unless you plot a series of small goals that will help you achieve these bigger ones. The small goals will help you on your way. Let's say you want to write a novel, but you have zero experience with creative writing. Worse still, you're not the most motivated person in the world. Unless you have to do something (such as work), you probably won't do it.

As you can imagine, writing a novel is going to be tricky for you. The standard novel is consists of 80,000 words. And for someone who is not used to daily writing, that's a lot. What you need to do is find an easy way of getting into the swing of things so that writing a novel doesn't become a cross that you can't bear.

So what do you do?

The first thing you need to do is instill the habit of writing daily. You can start with a short paragraph each day. A paragraph can be as long as you want it to be. Ideally, keep the chances of you failing to a minimum. It can be a single paragraph containing 10 sentences or a paragraph containing 3 sentences. If you go by number of words, you can aim for 100 – 500 words per day for the first week and slowly increase it from there.

A paragraph each day might not sound a lot, but it's a key part of the habit-forming process. You have a goal (a paragraph) and you have something relatively easy to do that connects to your bigger goal; mapping the route you have to take. Without this small goal, your big goal will continue to look overwhelming.

Get Rid of Extraneous Choices

Believe it or not, there are successful guys who eat the same thing for lunch every single day. Not only that, some of them including Steve Jobs and even Mark Zuckerberg, go so far as wearing the same type of clothes each time. Think Jobs signature black turtleneck and Zuckerberg's gray t-shirt.

The thing is, this makes a lot of sense. Successful men who eat the same thing each day aren't motivated by the delicious cuisine they can't get enough of, their primary motivation is instead the fact that eating the same thing for lunch each day means they've got one less thing to make a decision about.

When people are faced with choices, it can have a negative effect on the willpower. It can cause willpower depletion to set in. Everyday, people make a lot of decisions. This includes deciding what to have for lunch, what to wear, what movie to watch, and so on. And when there is such an abundance of choice, it's all of a sudden difficult for people to settle on a new habit and make it stick.

You might think it sounds boring to eat the same thing for lunch each day, but just think how efficient it can make your life. Just think of how much time you can save, plus the fact it's one less thing to worry about.

CHAPTER 4: LET'S BUILD UNSTOPPABLE WILLPOWER

You now understand what willpower is and why it's so important. You also now know how it can fail you and how habits help to shape it. Now let's get down to business and learn how to build unstoppable willpower.

Begin By Setting SMART Goals
SMART is an acronym that can be broken down like this:

- S - Specific
- M - Measurable
- A - Attainable
- R - Relevant
- T - Time-bound

SMART goals are popular and useful, because they help you to create goals you can envision and achieve.

Be Specific
Have you ever tried to achieve goals when you were younger but couldn't because they were so vague? Perhaps you've been guilty of doing the same thing.

When you say, "I want to lose weight," it's a commendable thing but it doesn't mean anything. How much weight do you want to lose? And when do you want to lose it by?

By asking and answering these questions, you're getting to the nitty-gritty of things. You're being specific by setting targets and deadlines.

You might say, "I want to stop eating donuts," but that statement alone is not enough. You need to be specific: What will you replace donuts with?

Being vague about your goals lets the demon of procrastination enter the room. You keep putting things off because you have no clear idea about targets and deadlines.

Be Measurable
Ever been good at data crunching? Well, you don't need to be good at analytics. But you do need to find a way of measuring your results. Otherwise, you won't know how far you've come, and how far you still need to go. You also won't know what parts of your tactics have been successful so far, and which haven't.

It's easy to measure goals, such as weight loss goals. You simply need to step on the scales every week or so.

If you're writing a book, maybe you could keep track of your word count. Whatever your goal is, it's important you find a way to track your progress.

Be Attainable
For this one, you need to ask yourself a few questions. How will you go about accomplishing your goal? How realistic is this goal? Let's say you want to go jogging

for thirty minutes each morning before work. Is this a realistic goal? Or would it be better if you went jogging for, say, fifteen minutes instead? And what if you're bad at getting up early? How are you going to overcome that particular problem?

How attainable your goal is largely comes down to how realistic it is. It's not possible to do everything. Your goal must be big, and it must be something you dream about. But it must still be something you can achieve within the timeframe you set.

Be Relevant
The goals you set needs to have relevance to your life, as well as to the other goals you set. It's no use setting a goal that doesn't harmonize with the rest of your life. For example, if you have a wife and children but your goal will take you further and further away from them, how does that work?

For a goal to work, it must be in accordance with your other long-term goals. If a long-term goal of yours is financial security for your family, but your new big goal is to quit your job and travel the world for two years, it clearly isn't relevant because it doesn't match up with your other long-term goal. Pick a goal that is worthwhile, and which will add value to your life.

Be Time Bound
Ever said that "someday" you'll do this or that? Maybe you've told friends that someday you'll open up your own business. Maybe you've told them you'll travel the

world. Maybe you've told them that someday you'll become a vegan. Someday - but not yet.

The problem with "someday" is it's an illusion. It doesn't exist. When you say "someday," you're referring to an abstract idea in your mind. It isn't based in reality. It's a specter.

As a consequence, someday never arrives. You're forever stuck where you've always been, and your dreams remain unfocused and neglected. They're just wisps of air, drifting into the ether.

It's really crucial to set deadlines. Deadlines are everything. Without them, you've got nothing to aim for. You can take a week or a month off from your goals because they're not due until sometime in the far-off future.

Deadlines keep you focused. They remind you of how far you've come, and how much there is left to go. Creative people in particular hate deadlines. But deadlines impose discipline, which is important if you are to achieve your goals in this lifetime!

CHAPTER 5: PERSEVERANCE, RESOLVE AND PATIENCE

How do you react when something unexpected happens and it threatens to disrupt your plans and cause a major delay? Let's imagine you're a freelancer who works from home, and who relies on the Internet. You've got a deadline today, and you've started work early. But just as you were hitting a stride, the Internet went off.

You check your router. Everything is fine your end. You call your Internet provider, who tells you there is an issue in your local area and that they're working on it. It could take up to eight hours to resolve. How do you react? It's easy to get annoyed and upset. It's easy to stomp around the house, cursing. However, if you're aiming for unstoppable willpower, this isn't the right way to respond. Instead, you need to have perseverance and patience.

Patience isn't easy to come by. It's a hard skill to develop. Today's world is very fast-paced and many times people feel they need things to happen right now. They can't wait 8 hours for the Internet to come back on. They need it right now.

But look, unstoppable willpower isn't going to come overnight. It's not an instant thing. It happens over the course of a few months as a result of the small decisions you make. You will have to do a lot of waiting.

There are a couple of things you can do to help sharpen your patience and resolve. For example, you can learn to accept that in life there will be delays. They're inevitable. But you need to use the delay to your advantage as much as possible.

Let's return to the freelancer who was stranded without the Internet for eight hours. The best way to react in this situation is not to get angry and throw a fit. Nor is it the time to go back to bed for a few hours, or lounge around in front of the TV. The best way to react is to use the spare time productively. Maybe there is a job you can do in the meantime that doesn't require the Internet. Maybe there are some household chores that you need to catch up on. Or perhaps you could use this time to do the grocery shopping today instead of tomorrow.

Delays happen. You will be made to wait. But what gives people the winner's edge is how they respond to these unexpected delays.

If you're stuck in traffic, download an eBook on your phone or Kindle and do some reading. Or maybe you could spend the time drafting a business idea you've always had inside your head but never put down to paper.

Delays are not the end of the world. Once you start associating a delay with a lot less pain, you can think with a clear head and how you're going to use your new spare time to your advantage.

Perseverance and The Environment

Your surrounding environment envelops you. Look around you and you will see it. It's everywhere, and no matter how many times you move around it's always there. Our environment doesn't go away. You can swap it for a new one but it's always there.

In light of this, think about how much your environment affects you. As a consequence, it's easy to blame your environment for the things that go wrong in your life, as well as the decisions you make.

For example, if you put on weight, you might be tempted to shift the blame from yourself to your environment. It's not your fault that you have to work such long hours that, when you do get home, you have no time to cook dinner. However, blaming your environment like this is misguided, and it will take you further and further away from your goals.

It's like when unsuccessful people look on with jealousy at successful people. They say the reason they're not successful is they had a rubbish upbringing. Unlike the successful people, who were all born with a silver spoon in their mouths. As you can see, indulging in this blame game says more about you and your mindset than it does about your environment.

And if you want to see examples of successful people who came from a much worse environment than you, all you need to do is Google. NBA All-Star Jimmy Butler was kicked out of his home by his own mom when he was just 13. And then there's Oprah Winfrey and her struggle while growing up. You'll be amazed.

You're not a product of your environment. You're a product of your mindset. Your environment doesn't decide your destiny. Your mindset does. Yes, coming from a poor background means it takes longer to get to the top than someone who was given a million dollars by their family. But this is where perseverance, resolve and patience come in.

Sometimes you have to juggle two rubbish jobs when you're young so that you can pay the bills. But it doesn't always have to be like this, not if you use your spare time wisely.

People who get to the top are not defined by their background. They are defined by their mental toughness, resolve, perseverance, patience and above all else, their work ethic. If you have these qualities by the bucket load, you will reach the top before those who got a head start in life, but who don't possess these qualities.

You'll hear successful people say that they're not particularly talented at anything. They just work harder than everyone else.

These qualities - mental toughness, resolve, perseverance, patience, work ethic - will sharpen your willpower so that it truly becomes unstoppable.

CHAPTER 6: SELF-CONTROLA ND SELF-DISCIPLINE

Self-discipline can be defined as making yourself do what needs to be done and self-control as refraining from what you shouldn't do.

Self Discipline
Ever put something off until the moment you had to do it? Most people have. People would rather procrastinate instead of doing something they know would benefit them.

Why is this?

It's because most people associate more pain with doing the task than with putting it off. Until eventually, of course, time runs out and they know they have to complete the task. At this point, there is more pain associated with not doing the task than with getting it done.

People who have remarkable levels of self-discipline know the importance of getting something done now. They're all too aware of how much pain they would suffer if they continued to put something off.

Freelancers need to have high levels of self-discipline if they're to keep on living the freelancer life. If self-discipline isn't your forte, you can't be a successful freelancer.

If a freelancer repeatedly chose not to work each morning, they're teaching themselves a very bad habit, and their willpower will remain weak. Remember that your habit will have a major impact on your life. The more you do something; the more it becomes second nature to you.

Self-discipline means getting stuff done first before relaxing.

A good way to tighten your self-discipline is to picture how great you'll feel when you know that a particular task is completed. What are the benefits of completing tasks as soon as possible?

1.) You'll have more free time

2.) You'll have less stress

3.) It won't be on your mind any longer

As you can see, all of these things will bring you a lot of pressure. Putting the task off, on the other hand, will bring you more pain. Such as:

1.) You'll get stressed as the deadlines nears
2.) You'll find it hard to enjoy anything because you know that the task still needs to be completed

3.) When you do the task, you'll feel rushed because the deadline is now so close. As a consequence, your work won't be your best. Worse still, you might have to do two or even three things at the same time.

The more you choose not to do something, the more you tell your brain that you're undisciplined, and the more it will pick up these undisciplined habits.

Self-Control

At some point in your life, you might have met someone who was a shopaholic. Shopaholics are a product of the consumerist generation. Someone created the credit card, and the credit card activated the shopaholic gene in a good number of folks.

When someone starts rationalizing their purchases and spending habits, you know they've got it bad.

"I need this new dress because I have a networking event on Friday, and I can't wear the same dress that I wore to a networking event last week in case the same people show up."

Most of them would explain away why they need several different bags for different occasions. And how they need different clothes because they can't wear the same thing each time. "You can't take this handbag into a club," they would say.

For some, shopping isn't a mere hobby. It's the way they connect with the world. It's their way of finding their own self-worth and identity. And when this happens, they find it hard to distinguish what they want from what they need.

People who have this problem likely wouldn't admit they have a problem at all. But once they finally realize that their spending habits is ruining them financially or that it's becoming problematic, they can drastically change.

It often takes something big to get people to change. It's like people who drink too much. For a while, they have no self-control. They'll get wasted at the weekend, but they won't admit they have a problem, nor will they cut back. They'll admit that the hangover is nasty, but they're not nasty enough to get them to rethink their lifestyle.

However, the moment they experience a major health scare is the moment they finally begin to exert self-control and examine their drinking habits. "I need to cut down," they'll say. The health scare has shaken them up, and this is often what it takes to get people to exert self-control over their behaviors.

Even though at some point, people will reach a breaking point causing them to ditch bad habits. It's important not to wait for the bad habit to reach a breaking point before making a change. By then, it might be too late. And even if it isn't, so much time is already wasted.

When you have habits that are out of control, you need to take a look at the underlying causes of your habits. Why? Because your aim is to retrain your habit, and to do this your must examine the reasons why you keep turning to excessive shopping, alcohol, gambling, or whatever vice you have that you can't control.

If you don't understand the triggers and the reasons, you can easily relapse even if you have started to make a change.

When you try to exert self-control, you need to stop looking at the symptoms and the effects, and start looking at the causes.

It's like when going to the doctor's office because you're sick. The doctor gives you a pill and sends you on our way. But this pill isn't addressing the cause. What you need the doctor to do is give you a preventative measure that will stop the problem from occurring in the first place. For example, he could recommend a better diet.

When it comes to mastering self-control, this is what you should do: address the underlying causes. Ask why you can't stop gambling. Do you gamble because you love the thrill? Do you need to win big money in order to feel invincible?

If so, it's important to find other ways to make yourself feel good that aren't so costly.

CHAPTER 7: WILLPOWER AND DECISION-MAKING

The amount of willpower you have is going to affect the kind of decisions you make during a day. When you are alert and fresh, you tend to make your best decisions that are good for you. This is just common knowledge. And when you're tired and "out of it," you're likelier to make some pretty terrible decisions!

The Italian neo-realism movie The Bicycle Thieves is a great example of how our ability to make decisions can fall apart. At the start of the film, the protagonist needs a bicycle for his new job. To get one, he must sell a few belongings. Unfortunately, his bike is then stolen.

The scene is set for a movie about a father and his son trying to locate the stolen bike. As the movie wears on, the father and son grow more desperate and tired. And as they do, their decisions become outrageous - they're clearly the result of a desperate and tired mind!

By the end of the film, the father is so desperate and low on hope and willpower that he splashes the last of his cash on a big meal for himself and his son.

Unconscious Decision-Making And How It Impacts Willpower

Any decision you make is connected to how much willpower you have at the present moment. If you have a small portion of willpower, you'll probably be tempted to break your diet momentarily and eat a piece of cake.

If you have a lot of willpower at the moment, you'll be able to abstain from temptation and stick resolutely to your diet. The more you make bad choices, the more your brain is trained to keep on making bad choices. It's just the way it goes.

When you're out shopping and don't have a great income, you're far likelier to make worse decisions than those who have a lot of money. This is because you don't have many choices - never have done - and this can seriously weaken your willpower. You begin to feel victimized - as though it's unfair that you can't spend and have nice things.

Watch Out For Defaults
Companies are all too aware of the science behind "decision fatigue," and they waste no time using it to their advantage. How? By setting their default options to the costliest ones.

You might see an expensive option first as you enter a store - online or offline. But it's too expensive. Of course you can't afford to buy it. You know that, and so do the store. So what happens next? In a store, the salesperson might first show you the expensive item - knowing full well it's likely out of your price range. After you've turned it down reluctantly, they'll show you an item that's less expensive.

It's still expensive, but because it's less expensive - and on discount - it suddenly looks more appealing when compared to the one you were just shown. Your willpower levels are so low by now you think "what the heck!" and hand over your cash. Bingo. The store has got you again. Decision fatigue makes you easy prey for the companies.

How To Prevent Decision Fatigue
The good news is that decision fatigue can at least be prevented. One way to do this is by fixing up your diet.

Have you heard of something called brain fog? Although brain fog is not a scientific term, it's the term you use whenever you feel out of it. You just can't kick your brains into gear. You feel tired, listless and morose all day long. You just can't summon the energy or the motivation to do anything. It's going to be one of those days. This is brain fog, and it can cause you to make poor decisions. The brain fog can be caused by a poor diet rich in bad fats.

See, when a lot of people think about bad fats, they think only about them in terms of how much weight these fats are going to put on their bellies and thighs. Rarely do they stop to think about how these bad fats could be working their way up to their brains. But they do!

Fats go to your brain. And when they do, they wreak havoc. They can make you tired, listless, and unmotivated. And all this can result in decision fatigue. It isn't just junk food that can cause people to make some screwy decisions - it's also a lack of food altogether. If you don't have enough glucose swimming around inside you, you'll find it hard to make the right decisions. Instead, your decisions will be impulsive and instinctive, and often irrational.

Eating well can improve your wellbeing, your willpower, and your decision-making.

It's crucial that you avoid making big calls when you're tired. If someone is pushing you to make up your mind about something but you're tired, politely tell him or her that you'll sleep on it. It's better to make a reasonable, logical decision with a refreshed, focused mind than with an exhausted one that isn't thinking straight.

Imagine having to go house hunting after a long day at work? You and your partner have been working 9-6, but in the evening you've got two houses to view. You're both exhausted and are finding it hard to focus on what the seller is saying to you. How can you expect to make the right decision in such circumstances? It's a much better idea to arrange house viewings at the weekend, when you're not working.

CONCLUSION

Most people believe their lives would change for the better if only they had more willpower. If only they had more self-control and more self-discipline, they would be able to achieve their dreams and live the life they want.

Then they would finally be able to return home from work and work on their side-business plan, rather than pop another cold one and sit in front of the TV. They would finally be able to cut out alcohol, say goodbye to the hangovers and get more stuff done.

Whatever dreams you harbor, you need willpower to help you achieve it. Build up your willpower reserve and live the life you want.

THANKS FOR READING

We really hope you enjoyed this book. If you found this material helpful feel free to share it with friends. You can also help others find it by leaving a review where you purchased the book. Your feedback will help us continue to write books you love.

The Smart Reads library is growing by the day! Make sure and check out the other wonderful books in our catalog. We would love to hear which books are your favorite.

Visit:
www.smartreads.co/freebooks
to receive Smart Reads books for FREE

Check us out on Instagram:
www.instagram.com/smart_readers
@smart_readers

Don't forget your 2 FREE audiobooks.
Use this link www.audibletrial.com/Travis to claim
your 2 FREE Books.

SMART READS ORIGINS

Smart Reads was born out of the desire to find the best information fast without having to wade through the sheer volume of fluff available online. Smart Reads combs through massive amounts of knowledge compiles the best into quick to read books on a variety of subjects.

We consider ourselves Smart Readers, not dummies. We know reading is smart. We're self taught. We like to learn a TON about a WIDE variety of topics. We have developed a love for books and we find intelligence attractive.

We found that each new topic we tried to learn about started with the challenge of finding the pieces of the puzzle that mattered most. It becomes a treasure hunt rather than an education.

Smart Reads wants to find the best of the best information for you. To condense it into a package that you can consume in an hour or less. So you can read more books about more topics in less time.

OUR MISSION

Smart Reads aims to accelerate the availability of useful information and will publish a high quality book on every major topic on amazon.

Smart Reads hopes to remove barriers to sharing by taking the copyright off everything we publish and donating it to the public domain. We hope other publishers and authors will follow our example.

Our goal is to donate $1,000,000 or more by 2020 to build over 2,000 schools by giving 5% of our net profit to Pencils of Promise.

We want to restore forests around the globe by planting a tree for every 10 physical books we sell and hope to plant over 100,000 trees by 2020.

Doesn't it feel good knowing that by educating yourself you are helping the world be a better place? We think so too...

Thanks for helping us help the world. You Smart Reader you...

Travis and the Smart Reads Team

WHY I STARTED SMART READS

Every time I wanted to learn about something new I'd have to buy 20 books on the topic and spend way too long sorting through them and reading them all until I arrived at the big picture. Until I had enough perspectives to know who was just guessing, who was uninformed and who had stumbled upon something remarkable.

I wished someone else could just go in and figure that out for me and tell me what matters. That's how smart reads was born. I want smart reads to be a company that does all that research up front. Sorts through all the content that is available on each topic and pulls out the most up to date complete understanding, then have people smarter than me package the best wisdom in an easy to understand way in the least amount of words possible.

For example, I got a new puppy so I wanted to learn about dog training. I bought 14 different books about dog training and by the time I got through the first 5 and finally started getting the big picture on the best way to train my puppy she had grown up into a dog.

Yeah she's well behaved. She doesn't poop in the house. I can get her to sit and come when I call. But what if someone else went in and read all those books for me, found the underlying themes and picked out the best information that would give me the big picture and get me right to the point. And I'd only have to read one book instead of 15.

That would be amazing. I would save time. And maybe my dog would be rolling over, cleaning up after my kids and doing the dishes by now. That my friend, is the reason I started smart reads. Because I wanted a company I can trust to deliver me the best information in an easy to understand way that I can digest in under an hour. Because dog training is one of many subjects I want to master.

The quicker I can learn a wide variety of topics the sooner that information can begin playing a role in shaping my future. And none of us knows how long that future will be. So why not do everything we can to make the best of it and consume a ton of knowledge. And I figured all the better if I can also make a positive difference in the world.

That's why we're also building schools, planting trees and challenging ideas about copyright's place in today's world. Because as a company we have to be doing everything we can to support the ecosystem that gives us all these beautiful places to read our books. Thanks for reading.

Travis

Customers Who Bought This Customers Who Bought This Book Also Bought

Mastering Your Time: Learn How Successful People Enhance Productivity, Beat Procrastination and Do More in Less Time

Overcoming Procrastination: Proven Strategies on How To Improve Focus, Get Things Done and Achieve Your Goals

Unlimited Memory - Moonwalking with Einstein Steps to Photographic Memory

Develop Self-Discipline: Daily Habit to Make Self Confidence and Will Power Automatic

Self-Esteem Supercharger: Build Self Worth and Find Your Inner Confidence

Unlocking Potential: Master the Laws of Leadership

Success Principles: Techniques for Positive Thinking, Self Love and Developing a Powerful

Thrive As An Empath: How to Protect Against Psychic Vampires and Leverage Your Special Gifts

www.ingramcontent.com/pod-product-compliance
Lightning Source LLC
Chambersburg PA
CBHW062022280526
45787CB00005B/2197